# Two Ships Passing

*For Gord and Andra*

# Two
# SHIPS
*Passing*

## a play by Dave Carley

**SIMON & PIERRE**
A MEMBER OF THE DUNDURN GROUP
TORONTO · OXFORD

Author photo: Michael Lee
Printer: Webcom Ltd.

Canadian Cataloguing in Publication Data

Carley, Dave, 1955–
Two ships passing
A play
ISBN: 978-0-88924-282-1
I. Title

PS8555.A7397T96 1999        C812'.54        C98-931575-4
PR9199.3.C37T96 1999

1    2    3    4    5        03    02    01    00    99

THE CANADA COUNCIL | LE CONSEIL DES ARTS
FOR THE ARTS | DU CANADA
SINCE 1957 | DEPUIS 1957

We acknowledge the support of the **Canada Council for the Arts** for our
publishing program. We also acknowledge the support of the **Ontario Arts Council**
and the **Book Publishing Industry Development Program** of the **Department of
Canadian Heritage.**

Care has been taken to trace the ownership of copyright material used in this book.
The author and the publisher welcome any information enabling them to rectify
any references or credit in subsequent editions.

*J. Kirk Howard, President*

Printed and bound in Canada.

Printed on recycled paper.

| Simon & Pierre | Simon & Pierre | Simon & Pierre |
|---|---|---|
| 8 Market Street | 73 Lime Walk | 2250 Military Road |
| Suite 200 | Headington, Oxford, | Tonawanda, NY |
| Toronto, Canada | England | U.S.A. 14150 |
| M5E 1M6 | OX3 7AD | |

*Two Ships Passing* premiered at Theatre Aquarius, Hamilton, on February 16, 1998. The cast and production crew were as follows:

| | |
|---|---|
| ANNA BREGNER | Gina Wilkinson |
| WESLEY MARSHALL | Ric Reid |
| JASON BREGNER | Jason Jazrawy |
| | |
| Director | Christopher McHarge |
| Set and Costume Designer | Dennis Horn |
| Lighting Designer | Mark Schollenberg |
| Sound Designer | Michael Stewart |
| Stage Manager | Barbara Wright |
| Production Director | Stephen Newman |

*Two Ships Passing* was next presented at the Carnegie Mellon Showcase of New Plays, Pittsburgh, Pennsylvania, in July, 1998. The cast consisted of Angelina Fiordellisi (ANNA); Joe Olivieri (WESLEY); and Matthew Fletcher (JASON). Sally Han directed and Lori J. Weaver was the stage manager.

**Characters:**
Anna Bregner, Age 42
Jason Bregner, Age 23
Wesley Marshall, Age 42

**Time:**
The very near future. June.

**Place:**
Act One — Anna's chambers at the courthouse. Friday morning.
Act Two — Wesley's office at the church. Sunday noon.

**Set:**
The set is pretty much the same for both acts, with only cosmetic changes during the intermission. In Act One, Anna's office is messy; the desk covered with loose paper, files, etc. There's a head-of-state portrait (of the Queen), federal and provincial flags, some diplomas, and a bookcase with legal texts. There are two doors — one to the hall and the other leading to the courtroom. In Act Two, Wesley's desk is much neater; the flag is gone, the portrait is

of something vaguely and non-aggressively spiritual, the bookcase should have religious or sociological texts, and the window might have a bit of colour to it (but not a traditional full stained-glass treatment). Again, two doors — one to the hall, the other a closet. The desk and furnishings in both instances should be fairly impressive. It is also necessary to see the hall outside the office door.

**Style Notes:**
Sentences ending with (bracketed phrases) indicate that that portion of the sentence should/can be covered by the subsequent speaker. Sometimes these overridden portions are contained within one character's speech, indicating that the character overrides his own speech.

**Thanks to:**
Gillian Barber, Mary Lou Chlipala, Marc Côté, Jackson Davies, Angelina Fiordellisi, Matthew Fletcher, Frank Gagliano, Peter Grier, Sally Han, Dennis Horn, Frank Janesh, Jason Jazrawy, Andra McIntyre, Mary Jo McLaren, Bill Millerd, Joe Olivieri, Virginia Reh, Ric Reid, Greg Richards, Kris Ryan, David Storch, Iris Turcott, Brendan Wall, Lori J. Weaver, Gina Wilkinson, and Barb Wright. Thanks also to Theatre Aquarius, the Carnegie Mellon Showcase of New Plays, the Canadian Stage Company, Arts Club Theatre and Theatre on the Grand.
Very special thanks to Chris McHarge, for commissioning, dramaturging, and directing the premiere production of this play.


Playwright's agent:
Patricia Ney
Christopher Banks and Associates
6 Adelaide St. E., Suite 610
Toronto, Ont.
M5C 1H6
(416) 214-1155

# Act One

[ANNA *barrels into her office, flustered,*
*wearing her street clothes. She begins changing*
*into her judicial wardrobe.*]

ANNA    Damn him damn him to hell. Of all the —
where's my goddamn — of all the nerve —
the arrogance of him, the supreme supreme
the unmitigated the colossal — *(Pulls self*
*up.)* I don't care. It's that simple. I don't
care. *(A laugh.)* See I don't care. I'm calm.
I'm calm. All right I'm calm.

[ANNA *slams her purse down. She then*
*begins trying to get her robe on. She's definitely*
*not calm.*]

I'm calm. Calm. I'm the calmest judge in
the country. The calmest damn judge in
the goddamn calmest land how the living
hell do you get into these things! *(She*
*stops struggling.)* Rise above this! Rise!
RISE woman! He's just a man. A very low
and scabrous blast-from-the-past man and
I am ...

[*There is a knock on the door.*]

*(Suddenly very serious.)* I am a judge. I am a
modern judge. A thoroughly modern ...
*(Seems calm.)* judge.

[*Another knock.* ANNA *rushes to the mirror. Final primp — this is both for vanity and to ensure the appearance of judgeship. She then perches on her desk. She realizes that the pose is somewhat unjudicial, so she rushes around to her desk and sits. She gets the bright idea to half turn her chair away from the door and there she poses, reading something exceptionally important-looking.*]

I am the judge. And a good judge, too. *(Then, deep breath:)* Come — in.

[JASON *enters, in casual dress. He is holding flowers.* ANNA *motions "quiet" without looking. For a moment* ANNA *finishes "reading" her document. She turns with great deliberation.*]

|  |  |
|--|--|
|  | Oh for God's sake. |
| JASON | (What) |
| ANNA | Jesus Murphy. *(Bangs her head.)* Aw damn. |
| JASON | *(Pause.)* Do you want to take this from the top? |
| ANNA | No! *(Grabs him, yanks him in, checking hallway.)* I was just expecting someone else — from work — a work person (I mean) |
| JASON | You haven't seen me since Christmas and all I get is "Jesus Murphy" and "Aw damn" and … *(Bangs head.)* |
| ANNA | Sorry. You're right. Jason — it is good to see you, welcome, welcome, very good to see you, a nice — surprise — a lovely one — |

[JASON *thrusts the flowers towards* ANNA *and she leaps back.*]

|         |                                                      |
| ------- | ---------------------------------------------------- |
|         | Get them away from me!                               |
| JASON   | (What?)                                               |
| ANNA    | They're stolen!                                       |
| JASON   | (How do you know)                                     |
| ANNA    | *(Kisses him.)* Welcome home. *(Swats him.)* I'm serious, Jason — if those were government property five minutes ago... They look like they're from the front bed. They look Federal. I'm sorry I didn't come to the bus station to get you — |
| JASON   | That's okay, you're busy —                            |
| ANNA    | I've got a sentencing this morning —                 |
| JASON   | I took a taxi home —                                  |
| ANNA    | What's wrong with your legs!                          |
| JASON   | There's nothing wrong with my legs. I had three suitcases. *(Of her robe:)* Very nice. |
| ANNA    | I look like a tea cosy. You look tired.               |
| JASON   | (No)                                                  |
| ANNA    | I was worried your finals would wear you out — you seemed pretty wasted at Christmas. |
| JASON   | I did?                                                |
| ANNA    | Though I guess there were mitigating circumstances. I mean, it's not as if you were actually sleeping at night. But I do worry about you getting run-down. |

[JASON *is looking doubtful.*]

|         |                                                      |
| ------- | ---------------------------------------------------- |
|         | I do! Hey — I'm being maternal here, help me.        |
| JASON   | Exams were a breeze.                                  |

[ANNA *takes the flowers.*]

|         |                                                      |
| ------- | ---------------------------------------------------- |
| ANNA    | Women don't fall for the flower thing. But thanks.   |

[ANNA *kisses* JASON, *then tosses the flowers in her desk drawer.*]

JASON       Mom!
ANNA        They're stolen!
JASON       Why do you automatically assume I stole
            them!
ANNA        Okay — where'd you buy them.

[JASON *hesitates:*]

Guilty.

JASON       That's not how the burden of proof works.
            First you have to tell me why you think I
            stole them —
ANNA        And then you'll admit you did.
JASON       Okay but they're not from the courthouse.
            You have gotten tough.

[ANNA *hugs* JASON.]

What's that for.
ANNA        I'm really, really proud of you.
JASON       You are?
ANNA        You've worked so hard and all you ever got
            from me was razzing: "Go into something
            useful."
JASON       Like social work boy that's really useful
            (nice advice)
ANNA        And "Don't be a goddamn capitalist" —
            how many times did you get that?
JASON       (A million)
ANNA        And I have to be perfectly honest, I really
            didn't think you had the brains for business.
            Well, your father was no rocket scientist!
            He was *(Knocks on desk.)* hello hello. And

you have to admit your teen years weren't
exactly covered in glory. But you did it, you
stuck to it, you aced it — did you ace it?

[JASON *indicates he did.*]

How did your job interviews go?
*(Remembers; looks at watch.)* You can tell me
later. *(Starts pushing* JASON *out.)* You
want the car?

|          |                                                        |
| -------- | ------------------------------------------------------ |
| JASON    | When do you have to be in court?                       |
| ANNA     | They'll beep me any second. *(Holds out keys.)* Here.  |
| JASON    | Actually, I thought I'd walk back home — I've been on the bus since (seven and) |
| ANNA     | You didn't tell me how your interviews went. Why are you avoiding the subject? |
| JASON    | They went fine!                                        |
| ANNA     | When do you start?                                     |
| JASON    | What do you mean.                                      |
| ANNA     | When — do — you — start — your — job. You did get a job. |
| JASON    | I got offered the position I wanted at the end of my first interview. I start Monday. |
| ANNA     | Aw honey, you should've phoned and told me. Who with? *(Pushing him towards door:)* But look, why not tell me all this at lunch. Do you want to do lunch. And dinner. You can tell me then, too. You could tell me now, but I'd rather hear it when I'm not court-bound. I want to savour it. We'll celebrate tonight. Will you be home for dinner or do you have a date? |
| JASON    | I've been in town a half hour!                         |
| ANNA     | What about that noisy thing?                           |
| JASON    | (Noisy?)                                               |
| ANNA     | The Shrieker.                                          |

| | |
|---|---|
| JASON | *(Pause.)* (The Shrieker) Naomi? |
| ANNA | You didn't bring her home with you? |
| JASON | No. |
| ANNA | Thank God, I'll get some sleep! Why didn't you bring her — does the poor thing still have exams? |
| JASON | Naw, I dumped her. |
| ANNA | Pardon me? |
| JASON | (I dumped her.) |
| ANNA | I heard you the first time. Jason: I didn't raise you to "dump" people. *(Beat.)* You didn't say who hired you. |
| JASON | It's a bank. |
| ANNA | I didn't raise you to work in a bank, either. |
| JASON | It's a Swiss bank. |
| ANNA | Why would you go work for a Swiss Bank!? What's wrong with our banks!? |
| JASON | It's a chance to travel. |
| ANNA | What — we embarrass you? You want to get away from us? |
| JASON | I'll be based in Toronto. Maybe New York. It's a Swiss Bank but I'm working here. |
| ANNA | Why not a Canadian bank and work there? Those Swiss Banks aren't exactly on the up and up. If you're going to launder money, at least do it domestically. Toronto? |
| JASON | Ninety percent sure. |
| ANNA | That's so far away. |
| JASON | No it's not. |
| ANNA | Well it's not here. |
| JASON | You can come every holiday and stay with me. |

[WESLEY *has arrived at the door to*
ANNA's *chambers. He's dressed in civvies —*
*jeans, a sports jacket, sunglasses perhaps. He*
*has flowers. He adjusts his jacket and is poised*
*to knock when he hears voices.*]

| ANNA | You'll be too busy dumping people. Okay, so I'll make you a great supper. *(Kisses him.)* And I really am proud. *(At the door.)* I didn't feel I could say this when you were seeing Naomi. But really, honey, a mother should never hear her son's girlfriend having an orgasm. |
|---|---|
| JASON | God Mom — you're (embarrassing me) |
| ANNA | How'd you think I felt! Every night, all Christmas holiday, listening to Noisy shriek down the wallpaper. Lying there, wondering: how liberal should a sleepless parent be? And even worse: worrying that she's faking. |
| JASON | I'll make sure my next girlfriend is quieter. She wasn't faking. |
| ANNA | Oh, I'm sure she wasn't. |

[ANNA *opens the door; sees* WESLEY; *slams the door shut in his face.*]

But — but how would you know?

[ANNA *is standing in front of the door, barring* JASON *from leaving.*]

| JASON | She told me. I'll see you at lunch. |
|---|---|

[ANNA *doesn't move:*]

Mom?

| ANNA | Uh — uh we should talk about this. Honey. If Naomi told you she wasn't faking — she was. And even if she wasn't, and she told you she wasn't, you wouldn't really know if she was or she wasn't. Not for sure. You'd have to ask her best friend. It's like the situation with Quebec. |
|---|---|

[JASON *indicates total incomprehension.*]

You know, are they happy or aren't they? How the hell do we know? No wait — Quebec's the reverse. Naomi's faking orgasm — but Quebec's faking being frigid. And you really mustn't say "dumped." It reminds me of your father. I'll never understand how you can be so much like him when you barely knew him. It's nature triumphing over nurture, I guess.

JASON      Naw, all men are like that. We're dogs. I thought you wanted me to leave.

ANNA      This is far too interesting to cut short. All men aren't dogs. That's just a myth spread by the men who are.

JASON      Name two exceptions.

ANNA      That's too easy for words.

JASON      I'm waiting.

ANNA      What's the name of the Swiss bank? Does it have an actual name or do they keep that a secret, too?

JASON      Two men. Two.

ANNA      Bill.

JASON      Bill?

ANNA      Bill, the court clerk. Mind you, he's seventy. But Bill won't be "dumping" anyone.

JASON      Two.

ANNA      *(Pause.)* Ghandi?

JASON      Young men. Live ones.

ANNA      Wesley Marshall.

JASON      What made you think of him!?

ANNA      I don't know he just came to (mind)

JASON      He dumped you!

ANNA      Okay, maybe he's a bad example

JASON      He's the worst example!

ANNA      He wasn't that bad!

| | |
|---|---|
| JASON | How can you say that! He was even worse than that teacher you went out with. |
| ANNA | Which (teacher) |
| JASON | And the mortician. |
| ANNA | Which (mortician) |
| JASON | And don't worry Mom — I don't use words like "dump" in front of women. |

[ANNA *indicates herself.*]

You know what I mean.

[JASON *starts to leave again.* ANNA *grabs him.*]

| | |
|---|---|
| ANNA | No. Stay. |
| JASON | But if we're going to do lunch — |

[WESLEY *has moved off by now.*]

| | |
|---|---|
| ANNA | Is that how you dumped the Shrieker? Over lunch? Did she cry? God, I bet that one bellowed. *(Hugs* JASON.*)* I'm really really proud of you. Masters of Business Administration. Who'd a thunk it. All those years, when you were in high school, and I'd look out night after night and see you barfing on the front lawn. *(Serious:)* I know it wasn't easy for you. |

[ANNA *looks out the door and sees that* WESLEY *has gone. She leaves the door slightly open.*]

| | |
|---|---|
| | But off you go now. |
| JASON | Wait. What's this about it not being easy? Because I'm not mentally gifted, is that what you're saying? |

ANNA    No no. Because of the part-time jobs you had to take while you were at school. Because your mother was the only lawyer in the country to practise at a deficit. Now (shoo)

JASON    You're too big-hearted. People take advantage of you. And while we're being sappy — we are being sappy, aren't we —

ANNA    (Yeah)

JASON    I'm really proud of you, too.

ANNA    *(Steering* JASON *to the door:)* That's nice. That's really nice.

JASON    *(Stopping.)* My mom — a judge. After a lifetime of wearing Birkenstocks and spouting half-baked feminist rhetoric — Now you're a judge. *That's* ironic. That is irony isn't it?

ANNA    More like divine retribution. But we can (talk about it later)

JASON    *(Hugs her.)* Whatever — it's the essence of cool. You are the essence of cool. I only wish Gran could have seen you.

[*This stops* ANNA.]

ANNA    Gran? What do you mean.

[JASON *indicates the surroundings.*]

She knew it was in the works.

JASON    She'd have pissed herself if she'd seen this office.

ANNA    Yeah.

JASON    She might even have stopped worrying.

ANNA    She never worried.

JASON    She never stopped.

ANNA    What're you talking about.

JASON    She'd get up at night and pace, waiting for

me to come home. I wasn't always barfing
on the front lawn. A lot of times I'd be
sitting with her in the kitchen; me sitting,
her smoking and pacing and worrying. "I
wish your Mom would settle down." "I
wish she'd get a job with a pension."

ANNA    Well I've got the pension now and guess
what — it's indexed! And look — I even
have my own parking space. Not that I
care. *(Points.)* But see — first spot in.

JASON    That's not your car.

ANNA    Oh, I can't actually park there. There was a
bomb threat last month — some idiot was
going to blow my car sky high. So now we
let the defence lawyers use the spot. I knew
Gran worried. I'm sorry she subjected you
to it. It was a control thing. When
somebody tells you they're worrying about
you, that's what it is — control.

JASON    Like you were worrying about me at exams.

ANNA    I'm your mother!

JASON    She was yours.

ANNA    Don't you get legalistic.

JASON    *(Shrugs.)* So what's on tap for today? I
thought I'd watch (this afternoon)

ANNA    Aw, dull stuff. Just a sentencing. You wouldn't
find it interesting, now shoo, shoo —

JASON    *(Not moving.)* No major decisions or
anything?

ANNA    No no, we try to keep Fridays light. It's
June, a lawyer's thoughts turn to golf —

JASON    *(Hauls out piece of paper.)* Now, don't yell at
me.

ANNA    Would I ever yell at you?

JASON    You left this on the kitchen table.

ANNA    *(Snatching it back.)* DAMMIT! You
shouldn't be reading that!

| | |
|---|---|
| JASON | It was on the table. I couldn't (miss it) |
| ANNA | It's just in rough! |
| JASON | (I know but) |
| ANNA | I'm still feeling my way through it! |
| JASON | So you're not giving this today? |
| ANNA | God no. I've got a ton of time still. |
| JASON | Because I'd like to talk to you about it. |
| ANNA | Sure. After Monday. |
| JASON | Why after Monday? |
| ANNA | Because I deliver my ruling on Monday at ten. |
| JASON | I want to talk to you before then. |
| ANNA | Why. |
| JASON | I just think some of your — uh — |
| ANNA | Some of my "uh" what. |
| JASON | Some of your uh the way you are approaching uh — |
| ANNA | What about it. |
| JASON | I uh I'm not second-guessing you — you're the one in the robes, you're the one with the training — |
| ANNA | Yes I am. |
| JASON | But your approach — |
| ANNA | It's not *my* approach, it's the law. |
| JASON | It sounds a lot like you. |
| ANNA | Of course it sounds like me, I'm writing it. But it's not like it's an editorial. I'm just sifting what the lawyers said. In this case, the government's lawyer was high-priced and articulate. The lawyer for the woman seeking the injunction was a moron. So maybe the part you think sounds like me is actually just me helping the moron out. |
| JASON | At least tone down your opening line. |
| ANNA | Why. |
| JASON | You sound slightly biased. |
| ANNA | I don't have a biased bone in my body. |

| | |
|---|---|
| JASON | *(Reading:)* "The Premier is a fascist asshole"? |
| ANNA | Oh I'm not going to say that — that's my attitude. It's the subtext — you know, I'll be saying one thing, but my whole tone will be that of a judge who is profoundly anti-fascist anti-premier anti-asshole. |
| JASON | I still think we should talk about it. |
| ANNA | I appreciate your concern, but I really can't allow lobbying. |
| JASON | I'm your son! |
| ANNA | And I can just guess what your position is. *(Sighs.)* I wish I'd been handed stronger arguments! It's driving me nuts. |
| JASON | It's a big case. |
| ANNA | Too big too soon. And I didn't get any help from the lawyers. |
| JASON | Yeah, the woman's lawyer was pretty lame. "You can't deny someone surgery whose heart is screwing up before the law was passed because that's applying the law retroactively to previously existing organs." Phew. |
| ANNA | Yeah, my subtext that day? "Is there no quality control on lawyers!?" Though maybe it doesn't matter at this level — no matter how wisely I rule, the government's going to appeal. |
| JASON | But Mom: the government won't have to appeal if you rule in its favour. |
| ANNA | Shut up, I'm ruling against it. And it's not the issues that've got them freaked. The financial ramifications are immense. Oh, this'll go all the way to the Supreme Court. And the media coverage *(Groans.)* |
| JASON | If it's so big, why isn't the senior judge doing it? |
| ANNA | He's on sick leave. |

| | |
|---|---|
| JASON | Not heart problems I hope. |
| ANNA | No, thank God — that'd be a little too ironic. I've never shrunk from a challenge but there's something to be said for them surfacing in their own sweet time. I haven't even been here six months — I'm still learning procedure. Hell, I'm still trying not to trip on my bloody gown. *(Sees time; jumps.)* God, look at the time. Listen, you've really got to go. Are you sure you don't want the car? |
| JASON | I've got three days off. I can relax. Hang out with judges. I'll just wait here till they call you. |
| ANNA | I should take a minute or two to uh collect my thoughts. |
| JASON | You really don't want to talk about this. |
| ANNA | No. |
| JASON | The biggest decision of your career. |
| ANNA | It's just that it's so complex and I'm (distracted and) |
| JASON | I don't know Mom — it seems simple enough: an eighty-year-old woman needs a quadruple bypass. The government has just passed legislation that removes a number of procedures eligible for medicare coverage — and that includes fancy heart operations for anyone over 75. Am I right so far? |
| ANNA | *(Nodding.)* The woman has a name, by the way — Sophie Jamieson. |
| JASON | But the government isn't actually prohibiting her — Sophie — from having the bypass. |
| ANNA | No — they just won't pay for it — which is essentially the same thing. |
| JASON | But the point is: she could have the operation. |

| | |
|---|---|
| ANNA | She can't afford it. |
| JASON | She's poor? |
| ANNA | No. She owns a house. |
| JASON | Sell the house. |
| ANNA | That's not the point. |
| JASON | It's not. |
| ANNA | No. |
| JASON | I'll tell you the point: the government is poor. According to the papers, her operation would cost upwards of a hundred thousand and the province has decided it can put that money to better use elsewhere. Like paying down the debt. |
| ANNA | In what moral universe is paying off a debt a better use of money than saving a life? |
| JASON | If you pay down the debt you could feed more poor children. |
| ANNA | Oh, and they're really going to do that. The Premier's going to cut taxes for his golf buddies. |

[JASON *indicates contempt.*]

| | |
|---|---|
| | Don't snort at me. Look, I have to get ready (for court) |
| JASON | This legislation de-listing expensive surgery is a pragmatic response to our ongoing financial crisis. In the nick of time too — Mom, look at all the operations they can do now — we can just about live forever — but it costs money! And anyway, making a list of procedures not covered by medicare is more honest. |
| ANNA | Honest!? |
| JASON | It's only legislating something that's been going on all along. Do you really think doctors aren't already prioritizing who gets |

what level of care? Come on, Mom. Who's
a doctor going to operate on first: a forty-
year-old father of three who needs a bypass
— or eighty-year-old Sophie? He's going to
make a choice — according to *his* personal
standards. But aren't those decisions
something we should be openly debating?

ANNA    So Sophie Jamieson dies.

JASON    We have to cut back to save the system!

ANNA    Sophie's being cut right out!

[WESLEY *has returned. He eavesdrops
through the slightly ajar door and then leaves
again.*]

*(Thinks she gets it.)* Ah — I know what
you're doing. You're playing Devil's
Advocate. That's good. I need that.

JASON    *(Backing off now.)* Sure.

ANNA    Anyway, I've still got all weekend to hone
my arguments in whatever direction I end
up leaning — against. Right now I've got
more pressing concerns. I've got a
sentencing. Don't know why they haven't
beeped me. Maybe they don't know I'm
here yet.

JASON    The receptionist did. She sent me down
here.

ANNA    I guess they're just late then.

JASON    So who're you putting away this morning?

ANNA    A shoplifter. An old goat. *(Consults file.)*
Grant Foley. He managed to sneak a
portable TV right out of a mall on his
electric go-kart.

JASON    So what are you going to do?

ANNA    Suspended sentence.

[JASON *indicates he's not impressed.*]

I can't put him in jail! *(Consulting pre-sentence report:)* He's got no family here, his wife died two years ago — he's 82!

JASON    Is he senile?

ANNA    No, he's not "senile."

JASON    Maybe something snapped —

ANNA    If it did, it's snapping a lot. This is his third conviction in a year.

JASON    A three-time shoplifter deserves to have the book thrown at him. Period.

ANNA    I used to shoplift too.

JASON    Yes, you did a lot of things, but they aren't relevant (here)

ANNA    I'd wheel your carriage into the drugstore and stack formula under you.

JASON    You gotta let this go.

ANNA    We'd sail out with the loot while you distracted everyone with your gurgling and cooing — which, Jason, kinda makes you an accomplice.

JASON    *(Smiling.)* I'm still proud of you.

ANNA    *(Beat.)* That really means a lot.

JASON    *(Kisses her.)* And sooner or later I'll have you seeing the light. I'll be back at lunch. My treat.

[JASON *flings open the door to the hall and exits.* ANNA *is very tense — she's not sure if* WESLEY *is out there or not. When she hears no greetings in the hall she goes to door, looks up and down the empty corridor, and then shuts the door with relief.* ANNA *straightens up her appearance again and picks up the Foley file. She walks about with it, reviewing her sentencing.*]

ANNA            "Mr. Foley, the Court takes a dim view of
                citizens who shoplift television sets out of
                stores." *(Not in her sentence:)* In their
                government-subsidized go-karts. I rather
                think that makes accessories of us all — we,
                the Canadian taxpayers. So next time you're
                trying the old five-finger discount, use a baby.

                [ANNA *is near the door.* WESLEY *returns
                purposefully and knocks.* ANNA *freezes, then
                hurries back to her desk.*]

                One minute!

                [ANNA *arranges herself in the "studying an
                important decision" position, though not
                facing away from the door this time.*]

                Come in.

                [WESLEY *enters, holding flowers.*]

WESLEY          Anna?
ANNA            Yes — oh, it's you. Wesley — Marshall.
                *(Stands, holding out her hand.)* How very
                good to see you. *(Sits.)*
WESLEY          You sound like the Queen.

                [WESLEY *hands* ANNA *flowers.* ANNA
                *stands.*]

                I brought you these.
ANNA            Oh. Flowers.
WESLEY          I stole them.
ANNA            Not from out front!
WESLEY          They were off a casket.
ANNA            I didn't need to know that.

| | |
|---|---|
| WESLEY | No. I suppose you didn't. *(Pause.)* It's good to see you. How very good. |
| ANNA | Ditto. |
| WESLEY | It's been a while. |
| ANNA | Ten years. *(Makes a "yikes" sound.)* |
| WESLEY | *(With her, makes the "yikes" sound.)* |

[*They both give a short laugh. Then another short laugh at the fact they just did identical short laughs.*]

| | |
|---|---|
| ANNA | I was surprised to get your message today that you wanted an appointment. Unfortunately, you're a bit late and I'm due in court (any second now) |
| WESLEY | Your door was shut — |
| ANNA | Yes, I was *in camera*. But really, I've got a (sentencing) |
| WESLEY | That's why I'm here. To talk to you about Grant Foley. |
| ANNA | What possible concern would he be of yours? |
| WESLEY | He was a friend of my mother's. Not so much Grant as his wife. Who's dead. |
| ANNA | I know. |
| WESLEY | So's my mother. Dead. But this wasn't always the case. I mean, they were live friends once, but they're dead now. |
| ANNA | Yes, everyone's dead but I'm about to sentence a live one (and) |
| WESLEY | And my sister told me about your mother. I'm really sorry. She was a fine woman. Though she was never too keen on me. |
| ANNA | She was an astute judge of character. |
| WESLEY | But it was recent? |
| ANNA | Right before Christmas (but really I) |
| WESLEY | I'm sorry. |

| | |
|---|---|
| ANNA | Thank you for being sorry (but now) |
| WESLEY | Did she know you were being appointed to the bench? |
| ANNA | Yes. Apparently she was relieved I was going to get a pension. Now, I must (get in there) |
| WESLEY | There's something you need to know about Grant Foley. |
| ANNA | *(Holds up pre-sentence report.)* I know all there is to know. |
| WESLEY | But this will change things. |
| ANNA | This is not the place. You must know that. You shouldn't be here if (that's what) |
| WESLEY | But we're old friends. |
| ANNA | *(Exasperated.)* No, we're not. We're not old friends. In fact, we're not even friends. People throw the word "friend" around way too lightly. We're two adults who haven't seen each other in ten years. Our last contact occurred when you dumped me. And even that wasn't in person, as I recall. |
| WESLEY | Okay, Okay. Now do you want to hear about Grant? |
| ANNA | Make it quick. |
| WESLEY | *(Spinning the tease out:)* Mom always said Grant was a terrible lecher. But he was essentially my godfather. I mean, after Dad died he was sort of *in loco parentis.* |
| ANNA | This is very touching. |
| WESLEY | He took me to ball games, that sort of thing. Mom even got him to tell me the facts of life. Which, according to Grant, boiled down to: Don't get caught. |
| ANNA | There had better be a point to this. |
| WESLEY | Mom wouldn't let Grant in the house — that's how bad his reputation was with women. She'd make him stand on the front porch because she said morality must not only |

be done — it must also be seen to be done.

ANNA    It's the same with justice Wes! Ley! If
anyone knew you'd barged in here pitching
for Foley –

WESLEY    I made an appointment — that's hardly
barging.

ANNA    Mentally you are. You're doing a serious
barge.

WESLEY    I don't mean to. And I truly am sorry about
your mother.

ANNA    Don't change the subject.

WESLEY    I remember how close you were.

ANNA    We fought like cats and dogs. This is
highly improper. The fact you're Foley's
friend and you're in my chambers is enough
to blow the case out of the water. And me
with it. I'm surprised you don't know that.
Or maybe you do know and just don't have
enough respect for me to care. So I think
you should leave. Oh God, I suppose you
left your name at reception. Go back and
say you lied. God she probably saw you
bringing flowers — she'll think I'm being
bribed.

WESLEY    There's no dollar value to them.

ANNA    (Steering him out:) Out.

WESLEY    Is the reputation of the judiciary so low
your staff thinks a bouquet buys a
judgment?

ANNA    (Really falling apart.) I've done worse for less!

WESLEY    You have?

ANNA    Not judicially, sexually.

[WESLEY stops at this.]

You've got to go! (Pulling him the other
way.) Maybe you can cut through the

|         | courtroom if no one's there yet — make like you're a repairman. |
| WESLEY | You've done "worse for less, sexually" — fascinating. |
| ANNA | Actually, more for less. Listen, it was an unforgettable thrill seeing you but now you've got to go. Why are you smiling! |
| WESLEY | I'm being mean. I've got some good news. |
| ANNA | Good news, what good news. |
| WESLEY | Grant Foley's dead. |
| ANNA | He's dead. |
| WESLEY | You don't have to sentence him. |
| ANNA | I'll kill you. |
| WESLEY | Those were his flowers. |
| ANNA | I am definitely going to kill you. When did he die? |
| WESLEY | Four days ago. |
| ANNA | Nobody told me! |
| WESLEY | We only found him yesterday. |
| ANNA | Oh the poor man — he was lying there three days. |
| WESLEY | He lived alone. His daughter is in Vancouver and she couldn't get an answer when she phoned, so I went over. I found him in his bed. A stroke, apparently. This heat's so hard on them. The letter from his lawyer with the sentencing date was taped to his fridge. I didn't think his daughter needed to see that, so I took it down. The funeral was this morning. |
| ANNA | That's fast. |
| WESLEY | It's summer. |
| ANNA | You should've told me about it when you came in. You should've walked through that door and said, "Hello Anna, he's dead." Or even better — phoned the news in. Anonymously. |

| | |
|---|---|
| WESLEY | And miss teasing you? |
| ANNA | We have really strict guidelines. A judge can't entertain interested parties in her chambers. |
| WESLEY | I guess the prohibition on entertaining in your chambers doesn't apply to boyfriends. |
| ANNA | What's that supposed to mean. |
| WESLEY | When I was asking for you at reception there was a young man on his way here — with flowers. |
| ANNA | Oh. Him. (*Thinking fast.*) He's just a — a toy boy — boy toy. |
| WESLEY | Nothing serious, then. |
| ANNA | Oh no. A spring fling. |
| WESLEY | That's good, because he was hitting on the receptionist. |
| ANNA | It's Jason you dork! |
| WESLEY | I wondered if it was. It has been a long time. He was just — he must be |
| ANNA | Twenty-three. Just graduated. |
| WESLEY | Good for him. |
| ANNA | University of Western Ontario. |

[WESLEY *sucks in his breath.*]

I know, it's a country club. The tuition includes green fees.

[*They are both enjoying mock horror.*]

It gets worse: Masters of Business Administration.

[*They make horrified sounds, then laugh. The ice is broken.*]

You're absolutely sure Grant Foley's dead.

WESLEY    I delivered the death certificate to the
Crown Prosecutor while I was waiting for
you to finish with Jason. *(Of the flowers:)*
You better put those in water.

ANNA    I was going to let Foley off with community
service again.

WESLEY    Yeah, he liked that. His last judge sentenced
him to two hundred hours at the foodbank
— it gave him a real sense of purpose.

[ANNA *tosses* WESLEY*'s flowers in the
drawer with* JASON*'s.*]

You have Scotch in there?

ANNA    You want a (shot of Scotch)

WESLEY    Just curious — I just thought all judges had
Scotch in their drawers.

ANNA    Nah. Truth is, we really are a sober bunch.
*(A smile, and a tease.)* But you used to
have a little nightcap after closing the
store. Bloom's Furniture. You'd have a
glass of sherry and cookies. All by your
lonesome.

WESLEY    I was solitary back then. Still am. Only now
I don't see it as a character flaw. But it's not
good — because of the business I'm in.
Ministering.

ANNA    Because it's so social?

WESLEY    *(Nodding.)* The wedding receptions are the
toughest. They feel duty-bound to invite
the minister, but they don't really want you
there. Clergy has a prophylactic effect on
parties. *(Pause.)* You look great.

ANNA    Don't be ridiculous.

WESLEY    No — you look really fine.

ANNA    I have a grown son working for a bank.
How can I look fine?

| | |
|---|---|
| WESLEY | Judging obviously agrees with you. |
| ANNA | You don't know what horrors lurk beneath this gown. |
| WESLEY | I'll say. I mean — I wear a gown too. |
| ANNA | Oh, I remember. What's under yours. 'Course you always remember things from your youth being a whole lot bigger. *(Pause.)* But thanks for the compliments. I'd say thanks for the flowers too if you hadn't ripped them off a corpse. |
| WESLEY | I was going to write you a note when you were appointed. My sister — Jude — told me. I gather it was a bit controversial. |
| ANNA | There was some grumbling. I was too young, I hadn't been practising long enough, I was being made a judge in the same city I'd worked in as a lawyer. I was getting it because I was a woman. You know the tune. Well, you wouldn't — but there is one. Anyway, here I am — Ontario Court of Justice, General Division. But hey — congratulations yourself. Though I guess you didn't really have a choice — aren't you "called"? Maybe you didn't want to be a minister. |
| WESLEY | Oh I wanted this. And I think I was called. But it wasn't some ringing command from heaven — more like an e-mail with a lot of spelling mistakes. But it's the right thing. You see, I've been afflicted with this notion I can help people through faith. |
| ANNA | When I ran into your sister — when she was pumping me for info — she said, she did let out well she could hardly expect the dope on my personal life and not give something back, (she told me) |
| WESLEY | Jude told you about Parkdale. |

ANNA        I haven't breathed a word.
WESLEY      It's public knowledge. They know here — I
            had to tell them in my interview. What
            exactly did she say?
ANNA        You were sowing your seed on holy ground.

[WESLEY *groans.*]

            Well?
WESLEY      It's true, I had a church in downtown
            Toronto, there was a ruckus, I had to leave.
            End of story.
ANNA        That's all you're telling me!?
WESLEY      What people seem to forget about the
            clergy is that we have the same physical
            desires as — football players, or —
            Presidents. And we have nearly as many
            groupies. Every church has two or three
            excellent women of unimpeachable
            character who regard their preacher as some
            kind of sexual trophy. At Parkdale it was the
            organist — she chased me all over that
            church for two years!
ANNA        Until poor you eventually succumbed and
            had sex with her.
WESLEY      And her sister. The choir leader.
            Sequentially. The sisters grew disenchanted
            and it ended badly. I had to leave. And my
            reputation precedeth me here. They've put
            me on a three month trial — actually, it's
            up this Sunday. A no-sex-with-organists-
            type thing, but it's also to see how I preach,
            and how well I relate to everyone —
ANNA        You know, the no-sex rule is probably
            against the Charter of Rights.
WESLEY      Tell that to my hiring committee. I doubt
            any of them have had sex for forty years.

| | |
|---|---|
| ANNA | Is celibacy really so tough? |
| WESLEY | Yes! I think it's because I started so late. I'm like one of those old hot water radiators you forget to drain until halfway through winter. You feel the damn thing about February and think, well, this sucker's kinda cold, and suddenly you clue in — it's ready to blow! So you screw off the little bolt and sure enough, the thing starts spewing dirty water (all over the floor) |
| ANNA | Enough! |
| WESLEY | Or maybe it's just something about a woman in robes...All that lush material. The way it starts at the neck and kind of billows out, so much guesswork — what's behind curtain number two? Some Sundays — I'm up there preaching on caring or sharing and all I can think about is the organist's draped bosom. And in my mind's eye I'm striding down from the pulpit with an air of authority, like Moses coming down the Mount, but instead of making commandments I'll be breaking them and — You have a nice view. |
| ANNA | It's a parking lot. |
| WESLEY | But it's a nice parking lot. You're driving a BMW. |
| ANNA | That's one of the lawyers'. |
| WESLEY | But the sign says — *(Turns.)* How about lunch? |
| ANNA | You really have changed. |
| WESLEY | So — |
| ANNA | Oh, I don't know — |
| WESLEY | Just lunch. |
| ANNA | *(Pause.)* Okay. Just lunch. |
| WESLEY | But could you wear your robes? |

[*They laugh.*]

ANNA

I guess I am more confident now. It would have been hard to be less confident. I was chasing you all over the store and all you'd say was, "Falling in love is going to be like a long slow river and I have to go with the flow and it'll be a damn slow flow." And, well, it turned out you weren't so slow so maybe we were more like two ships in the night — except we did our fair share of bumping before we passed.

[*Pause. A thick one. Talking about the bad has reminded them of the good. They take a step towards each other but stop when there's a series of beeps from the intercom.*]

That's my cue. Bill the Clerk's waiting outside to escort me into court for the Foley sentencing.

WESLEY   But he's dead!

ANNA   I still have to bang the old gavel. The Crown will tell me the sad news — I'll have to remember to act surprised.

WESLEY   Lunch then?

ANNA   Sure. *(Looks at watch.)* It's eleven. Come back in an hour. *(Almost exits.)* Oh Lord, Jason. I said I'd — well — I'll change him — no that's not right — we'll have to take a raincheck, aw heck, I'm making Jason dinner, I'll make him something special, okay, I'll cancel him. When I get back. Maybe you could phone him and cancel for me. No, on (second thought)

WESLEY   I'll wait here for you.

ANNA   Don't you have anything to do?

| | |
|---|---|
| WESLEY | No. |
| ANNA | Okay, but don't give your name to anyone. If my secretary comes in, just act like you're not here. Tell her you're my brother. I'll be right back. |

[ANNA *exits.* WESLEY *smiles and watches her leave. As soon as she is out the door he goes to it and makes sure it's securely shut. He looks around the office and then goes immediately to* ANNA's *messy desk. He begins rooting about it until he finds* ANNA's *preparatory notes on the Sophie Jamieson case — the paper* JASON *had brought in earlier.*]

| | |
|---|---|
| WESLEY | Eureka. |

[*Just as* WESLEY *starts reading* JASON *walks in.* WESLEY *has his back to him.*]

| | |
|---|---|
| JASON | Who are you? |
| WESLEY | (*Shoves judgment in his jacket pocket; turns.*) Jason? |
| JASON | Yes. You're Wesley. |
| WESLEY | That I am. |

[WESLEY *and* JASON *shake hands; polite but cool.*]

| | |
|---|---|
| | This is an unexpected pleasure. |
| JASON | Uh huh. |
| WESLEY | You've certainly changed since I last saw you. |
| JASON | Uh you too. |
| WESLEY | I guess I have. |
| JASON | Where's Mom. |
| WESLEY | Sentencing someone to death. She'll be back |

|          | in a minute. *(Pause.)* I hear you're an MBA now. Congratulations. Got a job lined up? |
|----------|----------|
| JASON    | Bank. |
| WESLEY   | Right, a bank. |
| JASON    | Banks are bad, huh. |
| WESLEY   | No no no banks are fine. No, a bank — that's great. A big bank? I guess they're all big. |
| JASON    | It's Swiss. *(Pause.)* Why are you here. |
| WESLEY   | I was meeting your mother on a uh sub-judicial matter. We got reminiscing and now we're doing lunch. |
| JASON    | She's having lunch with me. |
| WESLEY   | I'm afraid you're getting cancelled. She's phoning you when she returns. She thought you'd be at home. |
| JASON    | I want to borrow her car. |
| WESLEY   | Oh. |
| JASON    | So she's double-booked. |
| WESLEY   | Wanna flip? |
| JASON    | We'll let her decide. |

[*Another pause.*]

| WESLEY   | The MBA — that's a pretty useful degree I guess. Your entire class get jobs? |
|----------|----------|
| JASON    | Pretty much. |
| WESLEY   | I've been back to school myself — since we last — crossed paths. I got a Bachelor of Divinity. I'm a minister. Of a church? I've been ordained. My class all got jobs too. Funny thing, one of them was hired by a bank. As a kind of stress counsellor. They've got him down on Bay Street, roaming the towers, praying with the (sharks) bankers. Taking confession. Sorry. I'm sure the Swiss are a lot more ethical. My friend is very |

|  |  |
|---|---|
|  | popular with the bankers. Believe it or not, there's a study, I think it's from New Zealand, it proves that mutual funds administered by bankers who pray regularly have an average yield 14 percent higher. Than those who don't. Pray. The image is a bit odd — buncha guys down on their knees praying for a bull market. Women, too. Lots of women MBAs now. And look at your Mom — a judge! |
| JASON | Yeah, she's done well. Despite everything. |
| WESLEY | (Mulling.) Despite (everything). (Pause.) Anyway, I'm back here now, at St. Peter's — the new church in the north end. Well, it's not that new, it was built in the 60s. When architects were optimists. Everything was designed like it was from "The Jetsons". The cartoon show? Lots of glass, arches. Anyway, optimism doesn't age gracefully. It's not a bull market for God these days. At least Organized God. God with dogma. God with pews. But Disorganized God — that's extremely bullish. God with crystals. Big big big. Maybe we should have the bankers praying for us. (Running down.) So. (Pause.) So. You're 23. You married yet? |
| JASON | No. |
| WESLEY | Dating anyone special? |
| JASON | No. |
| WESLEY | Ah. Playing the field. That's good. Get it out of your system before you look foolish getting it out. But be careful. It's dangerous out there. A lotta bad things going around, just keep a condom handy (in case) |
| JASON | Excuse me? |
| WESLEY | Of course — sorry — sorry, Jason. I counsel youth, well, any youth I can find. It's not |

[JASON *is gone.*]

|  | Well, now I feel old. |
|---|---|
| ANNA | Yeah. Who said kids were supposed to keep you young. |
| WESLEY | He told me about his job. |
| ANNA | You didn't get smart — |
| WESLEY | I'd never do that. I mean, I would do that, but only if he was my son. Of course, if he was my son he wouldn't be working for a bank. |
| ANNA | So I've failed. |
| WESLEY | No no I mean children always become the opposite of what you are. You're a left wing judge — so your son works for a bank. I'm a liberal clergyman so my son would be … *(Reaching for something.)* |
| ANNA | Celibate? |
| WESLEY | Touché. Anyway, Jason seems very poised, personable — |
| ANNA | Meaning I'm not? |
| WESLEY | Compared to when he was 13. |
| ANNA | You really didn't argue? |
| WESLEY | We were complete adults. And I wouldn't worry about him being such a little neo-con. |
| ANNA | Did I say I was worried? |
| WESLEY | Lots of men loosen up as they get older. Look at me. Remember how repressed I was when we met? |
| ANNA | *(Fondly.)* Repressed barely begins to describe it. |
| WESLEY | But you cured me. |
| ANNA | "I'll be a long, slow river." Hah. |
| WESLEY | I really don't think I said that. |
| ANNA | Oh yes you did. You asked me to the closing night party of Bloom's Furniture and when I said, "And after that?" you said, |

"We'll just go with the flow and it'll be a slow flow." And then you commenced to flow, for a (year and)

WESLEY       Eighteen wonderful months. *(Pause.)* I really hurt you.

ANNA         It was ten years ago, for God's sake. I've forgotten. I might have been a little hurt at the time.

WESLEY       I just didn't think that (it would work)

ANNA         I know what (you thought.)

WESLEY       (I wasn't ready)

ANNA         It was explained quite nicely in your note. It wasn't anything to do with me; you couldn't be a father to Jason and oh that made me feel a lot better, thank God it was nothing I did, it was all the kid's fault.

WESLEY       He hated me.

ANNA         Actually, he didn't.

WESLEY       I was useless with him.

ANNA         Yes, you were. But a lot of men are useless with their kids, big deal. It isn't usefulness that's required. It's presence. Being there. The important thing for Jason was he finally had a man around the house, which must've been a helluva relief for him after thirteen years of just his grandmother, and me on weekends. The duelling harpies. How could you have been so insensitive!

WESLEY       (I didn't mean to)

ANNA         You must've known, you must've! Jesus, Wesley, a week before you left, he'd asked you to go with him to that father-son hockey banquet — that's not a kid who's hating someone! That's a kid who's bloody excited that for the first time he can be like every other kid and YOU SAID YES — then a week later you slide a note under our door ...

| | |
|---|---|
| WESLEY | I don't know about the floor; I've developed a back thing. |
| ANNA | That's okay; my foot freezes up now. |
| WESLEY | What during (sex) |
| ANNA | Yeah, the minute I get going, it just goes thwonk and I'm pointing at the ceiling with my big toe, like a prima goddamn ballerina. |
| WESLEY | I know what to do for that. |
| ANNA | You do? |
| WESLEY | The deaconess had the same problem. I snore. |
| ANNA | When did that start! |
| WESLEY | I don't know exactly. Apparently I'm like a leaf blower. |
| ANNA | And you've been tested. |
| WESLEY | For snoring? |
| ANNA | Shut up. |
| WESLEY | Yes I've been tested; I had to, for insurance. I'm fine. |
| ANNA | Me too. |
| WESLEY | Okay. |
| ANNA | Okay. |
| WESLEY | Okay. |
| ANNA | So hold that thought till tonight. |
| WESLEY | Okay. |
| ANNA | Okay. Oh, the lights have to be a lot dimmer now. Candles are good. |
| WESLEY | Okay. |
| ANNA | So don't kiss me now. |
| WESLEY | I won't. |
| ANNA | Because if you kiss me now that's it. We're doing it right here, right now. Right on that — very — large — desk. |
| WESLEY | We'll wait till tonight. |
| ANNA | You don't have that much self-control. |
| WESLEY | For you I do. |
| ANNA | That's excellent. Because I've got a big |

|        | judgment coming up and I've got to work on it, and then Jason will be back in an hour for lunch and I don't want him barking at me about what to write — you're staring, don't look at me like that, what are you doing? |
|--------|-----|
| WESLEY | I'm just holding the thought. |
| ANNA | Hold it tighter. |
| WESLEY | Seven? |
| ANNA | Six. Let me get you the address. |
| WESLEY | I know where you live. |
| ANNA | Right. |
| WESLEY | *(Turning to leave:)* So you're glad I barged in? |
| ANNA | Yes, of course. Six o'clock. |
| WESLEY | Six. |
| ANNA | Five-thirty. |

[WESLEY *turns to leave; turns back.*]

| WESLEY | Maybe you could wear the *(Indicates robe.)* |
|--------|-----|
| ANNA | Get out! |
| WESLEY | See you tonight. |

[WESLEY *exits. He closes the door behind him and pauses.* ANNA *is at her desk. Outside the door,* WESLEY*'s smile suddenly turns to horror as he pulls the rough judgment from his jacket pocket. He shoves it into his jeans back pocket.*]

Oh God. Oh God oh God. I'll have to shove it back on her desk. Yeah, I'll slip it on (her desk and)

[*He seems to be about to knock on the door, but instead he opens it and strides back in.*]

ANNA
Sorry (I think I dropped something) *(Completely misinterpreting his return. Over him:)* Okay but Jason'll be back in an hour. That's not long. *(Grabbing* WESLEY.*)* But if I remember correctly you'll be able to do it four times by then. Or we could stop at three and have time for a smoke.

[ANNA *kisses* WESLEY; *he reciprocates.*]

Lock the door.

[ANNA *runs to lock the door to the courtroom as well.* WESLEY *is dashing over to the desk to slip the judgment back on.* ANNA *turns.*]

WESLEY
No no! You've gotta lock the door! Bill the Clerk could walk in! *(Runs back to lock the door.)* Okay okay.

[WESLEY *locks the door and runs back to the desk.* ANNA *has beaten him there. She is struggling with her robe.*]

ANNA
Damn damn can't get into it can't get out of it.

WESLEY
On the desk?

ANNA
Sure. *(Sweeping desk clear; lying back on the desk.)* Missionary?

WESLEY
What else is there?

ANNA
God I hope those locks hold. We'll have to be quiet. No yelling. I don't want any yelling.

WESLEY
I won't yell.

[*Various things are falling off the desk.*
WESLEY *is kissing* ANNA.]

ANNA

And I'm not going to fake anything. So
don't ask me after how it was, because I
don't want to have to lie so soon.

WESLEY

Shut up and kiss me.

[WESLEY *is kissing* ANNA. *Slowly her foot
rises to the ceiling.* WESLEY *is oblivious.*]

ANNA

Wes. Help Wes. Wesley, my foot, please —

[*Without looking,* WESLEY *reaches back and
starts rubbing the sole of her foot. It eases and
her leg returns.*]

Oh that's excellent. That's a real skill you've
picked up.

[ANNA*'s hands move down* WESLEY*'s
back. She comes across the wadded judgment
in his back pocket. She pulls it out.*]

Can we ditch the sermon. I can't have sex
with a sermon so close — or is it Foley's
eulogy or

[ANNA *is about to throw it on the floor,
but something catches her eye; it looks
familiar. She unravels it a bit; all the while*
WESLEY *is oblivious to this and madly
kissing her.*]

Hey. Hey. HEY!

| | |
|---|---|
| ANNA | For someone on probation with an unlocked door you're awfully candid about The Flock. |
| WESLEY | Why'd you come here. Go home. |
| ANNA | Funny — the last time I went to church the minister shook my hand and invited me to coffee hour. |
| WESLEY | You must've had a good laugh, watching them all nod off. Is that why you're here — to thank me for a good laugh? |
| ANNA | No. |
| WESLEY | Wait: you came to apologize. *(Points to eye.)* |
| ANNA | Why would I apologize for something you so richly deserved? But I do want you to know that I know that I shouldn't have decked you. I've always been four-square against humans decking humans. Judges, in particular, are not supposed to belt people. Especially the clergy. Even slimeball clergy. I want you to know I'm aware of that. |
| WESLEY | You are so ethically hip. |
| ANNA | Was that sarcasm? |
| WESLEY | It might have been. |
| ANNA | Well watch it — or you'll get a matching eye. I told you I know it's wrong. So now there's no doubt as to who has the ethics around here. Note *my* use of the word. Ethics. Note its application to *me*, as in wrongs done to *me*. Because I still don't know if you know how — how — sick, how |
| WESLEY | (I know) |
| ANNA | How incorrect, what a monstrous breach of trust it is to walk into someone's office and take her confidential (notes) |
| WESLEY | I KNOW! |
| ANNA | Do you!? It's kind of a pattern with you, isn't it. This betrayal thing. I don't know if |

one lousy black eye is enough to change
that. How is it?

WESLEY    As if you care.

ANNA    You're right, I don't.

WESLEY    Then why ask.

ANNA    I'm being polite. It looks awful.

WESLEY    Yes, and everyone was pretty darn curious
to know how I'd got it.

ANNA    Before they nodded off.

[*Pause while they both wait for the other to
apologize.*]

Well.

WESLEY    Well?

ANNA    Well, do we — meaning you — do you
have anything to say? Do you, for example,
do you want to apologize and ask me to
forgive you? Because if you were to ask or,
better yet, beg for forgiveness — I might.
Forgive. Now that I've seen your eye and
know that you're not blinded or pressing
charges, yes, I'm somewhat in the mood (to
forgive)

WESLEY    I'm the victim of violence here! Shouldn't I
be forgiving you? Gosh, it never occurred to
me to press charges.

ANNA    They'd never stand up in court. Okay. We'll
forgive each other at the same time. On the
count of three. One two three. I'm sorry I
hit you.

WESLEY    I'm sorry you did too.

ANNA    You apologize!

WESLEY    It wouldn't be honest.

ANNA    You just said you knew taking the notes was
wrong!

WESLEY    It was wrong but I was right to do it.

ANNA    "It's right to do wrong" — is this what
you're teaching now? Okay. Tell me one
thing. Out of the idlest of curiosity. When
you came to my office on Friday — did you
come to tell me Grant Foley was dead, and
you just happened to see my notes on
Sophie Jamieson — or all along were you
there to influence me?

WESLEY    Well I had to tell you about Grant, didn't I.
I couldn't let you sentence a corpse to
community service! And if Sophie came up
in conversation I was prepared to speak on
her behalf. Why not. Finding the draft
judgment on your desk — accidentally —
was a situation I hadn't quite (expected) aw
hell Anna — I came to your office because I
wanted to see you.

ANNA    Huh?

WESLEY    Yeah.

ANNA    Me the judge.

WESLEY    No, you the you.

ANNA    Hah — are you trying to tell me the little
"amour" you threw my way was (*A mock
throat catching*) real?

WESLEY    Yes.

ANNA    Hah — save your breath. I don't believe it.

WESLEY    I mean it.

ANNA    Hah.

[*But this has stopped* ANNA; *she probably
does believe him. At the very least, she would
like to.*]

Hah. Why.
[WESLEY *shrugs.*]

WESLEY    It was how I felt. I've come back to this city

where I spent my first thirty years being weird and solitary — but it's also the place where you are, where we'd had something wonderful, briefly. And I hoped we'd meet somewhere, just at random, sometime in the past three months, on the street or at the liquor store. And I'd say, casually, "Oh hello Anna," and you'd say warmly, or at least non-violently, "Oh hello, Wesley." And we'd be friends, adult-type friends or — or maybe we'd even start dating, adult-type dating. But the city's big and the random thing wasn't happening so I decided to force the issue.

ANNA    There are other single women in this city. I could give you Mary Jo Silcox's phone (number)

WESLEY    I spent thirty years here and the only thing that came out in the plus column was you. I'm serious. And when I walked into your office and saw you, wham, it was like the past ten years had never happened; you look just as fine to me as that first night when you came to my store. I wish I'd told you about my interest in Sophie's case. I know. I should have, of course I should have. But you have to believe me, the attraction part of it, that was real, that is real, that's why I was trying to call you all weekend.

ANNA    Every bloody half hour.

WESLEY    I had to tell you (that)

ANNA    It was weird!

WESLEY    You never answered.

ANNA    I've got call display. The first time you phoned it scared the living hell out of me — the display read "St. Peter". Five St.

nothing else. It'd fetch about what her operation will cost. She's got a fifty-year-old daughter living at home with her, she's developmentally slow, she's dependent on Sophie. But in order for Sophie to continue taking care of her she needs the operation so she can live, and to pay for that, if medicare won't — they'll have to sell her house. They'll be destitute! I can't let that happen. I won't let that happen.

[ANNA *is staring at* WESLEY.]

|          | What.                                          |
|----------|------------------------------------------------|
| ANNA     | Nothing.                                       |
| WESLEY   | You're staring.                                |
| ANNA     | You really like it here.                       |
| WESLEY   | Here.                                          |
| ANNA     | This.                                          |
| WESLEY   | Yes.                                           |
| ANNA     | Snorers and all.                               |
| WESLEY   | Yeah. I hope they let me stay. Today's the big day. The hiring (committee's) You're staring again. Plus you're smiling. |
| ANNA     | Am I?                                          |
| WESLEY   | I like your smile.                             |
| ANNA     | Do you.                                        |
| WESLEY   | Does the smile mean I'm forgiven?              |
| ANNA     | This is progress — you admit there's something that needs forgiving? Okay yes, I'm leaning that way. |
| WESLEY   | Good. You're smiling again.                    |
| ANNA     | Am I?                                          |
| WESLEY   | *(Pause.)* No wait — that was more like a leer. |
| ANNA     | The Bible says that forgiving can be very exciting. |
| WESLEY   | It does not say "exciting."                    |

| | |
|---|---|
| ANNA | But that's what I'm feeling so it must be. Exciting. |
| WESLEY | Now whoa — this is making me nervous. |
| ANNA | How nervous? |
| WESLEY | I never liked that smile. No Anna. Not here. |
| ANNA | I don't understand. What was fine in my office isn't fine in yours? |
| WESLEY | This is a very different situation. |
| ANNA | All the better to try out your situational ethics. Just a kiss. |
| WESLEY | You know we can't kiss; we'll have sex. |
| ANNA | No we won't. I have self-control. |
| WESLEY | No you don't. Neither of us do. But especially not you. |
| ANNA | Doesn't your door lock? No? What — they removed the locks as part of your probation? Kiss me. |
| WESLEY | I'm not allowed to. |
| ANNA | On Friday you were. You came bounding back into my office – |
| WESLEY | I was just going to sneak the judgment back on your desk. |
| ANNA | So when you started kissing me — what was that all about? |
| WESLEY | I was distracting you. I was prepared to do just about (anything) |

[ANNA *is looking vaguely violent again.*]

| | |
|---|---|
| | It was all tied together, Sophie, you — |
| ANNA | You're way too honest, Wes. You shouldn't have told me that. If I was a less forgiving person it might have pissed me off. |
| WESLEY | But it's — it's all mushed together — helping Sophie, liking you — we're humans, Anna: we're always blending |

selfishness and altruism. I mean, without
selfishness the altruism is a non-starter. And
there's nothing uglier than self-interest
without altruism. Thank God you've
stopped smiling.

ANNA           I'm thinking about the altruism stuff.
               *(Starts smiling again.)*
WESLEY         Where are you going?

[ANNA *has gone to* WESLEY*'s coat rack and
is getting his robe off the hanger.*]

ANNA           *(Of gown:)* Funny how ten years later we're
               both wearing gowns. I quite like these
               stripey flaps you have. Is it like the army —
               did you get these for courage under fire?
WESLEY         It's just decoration.

[ANNA *is putting his gown on.*]

Now what're you doing.

ANNA           Relax.
WESLEY         I can't relax. Someone might walk in.
ANNA           I'm just trying it on.
WESLEY         I'm still on probation.
ANNA           For what, five more minutes?
WESLEY         Well all right. I guess if the alternative is
               sex —
ANNA           Who says we're not having sex, too? You
               like women in gowns. I like being a woman
               in one. That's divine synchronicity.
WESLEY         Do you want to go somewhere nice — for
               lunch?
ANNA           Oh for sure. After.
WESLEY         There's a really smart cafe down the street.
               Let's go there and reminisce. Now. Anna: if
               (someone comes)

| | |
|---|---|
| ANNA | I'd rather stay here and "reminisce." Remember our first time? |
| WESLEY | It was over too fast to remember. I was lousy. I haven't improved. |
| ANNA | You were sitting on that unsold waterbed with your little bottle of sherry, wondering how the hell you could weasel out of the date you'd just made with me. You were going to weasel, weren't you. |
| WESLEY | Yeah. |

[WESLEY *has been edging to the door, but* ANNA *heads him off.*]

| | |
|---|---|
| ANNA | I forget what I was shouting when I ran back in the store — |
| WESLEY | "Take off your clothes!" |
| ANNA | Something like that. |
| WESLEY | I know why you're doing this. You're teaching me a lesson. Okay I've learned it. |

[ANNA *smiles.*]

| | |
|---|---|
| | What. Now what? |
| ANNA | I was remembering how — when you were talking about Sophie, I just remembered — well, that you have that side, that supportive, nurturing thing. And you had it long before it was trendy for men. There's something about a nurturing man that excites me. In a sincere kind of way. |

[ANNA *drops an article of clothing, her skirt, from under the robe.*]

| | |
|---|---|
| WESLEY | What's that. |
| ANNA | What's what. |
| WESLEY | That there. |

| | |
|---|---|
| ANNA | Oh that. |
| WESLEY | You just dropped that. |
| ANNA | I did? |
| WESLEY | It fell out. |
| ANNA | My robes don't breathe like this. Yours are positively airy. Interesting that yours should be so less constricting. But then I guess religion has more room to manouevre than the law. At least the way you practise it. |

[*Something else drops out: her blouse.*]

| | |
|---|---|
| WESLEY | This is neither the time nor place — |
| ANNA | And my office was? |
| WESLEY | Seriously: what if the Hiring Committee walks in. They're meeting right now. |
| ANNA | Where. |
| WESLEY | Well I think they went up the street I mean I think they're in the park but that's just across the road, they could come back here or they'll buzz me from the Session room. |
| ANNA | They'll buzz you? |
| WESLEY | Yeah, it's like picking a pope. You know — when the Cardinals vote they do that smoke thing? Well, we're Protestant — so we use technology. They'll buzz and I'll go see if they give me the thumbs up. |

[ANNA *hands her brassiere out from her gown.*]

| | |
|---|---|
| | Aw no (please) |
| ANNA | I read a scientific survey once about sex on Sundays. It said a woman is twice as likely to have an orgasm on a Sunday as any other day. |
| WESLEY | I never believe surveys. |

| ANNA | This one was by a university in New Zealand. God bless New Zealand. It must be wonderful to live in a country where they have the time to do studies on that sort of thing. Imagine being a volunteer. |
| WESLEY | What was the second best day? |
| ANNA | Thursday. |
| WESLEY | Let's wait till Thursday. |
| ANNA | Let's not. And actually, it wasn't Sunday as in all-day Sunday, it was Sunday afternoon. Before people get worrying about what they have to do on Monday. We can't let this opportunity pass. |

[ANNA's *panties drop*.]

| WESLEY | They're just up the street! |
| ANNA | Someone's always just up the street. I want to do it now. I've forgiven you. Forgiveness excites me. |

[ANNA *kisses* WESLEY *long and hard.
Then stops.*]

| WESLEY | Forgive me Father. |

[WESLEY, *with his free arm, sweeps his desk clear and lies back on it;* ANNA *climbs on top of him.*]

| ANNA | You really don't have any self-control. |
| WESLEY | Shut up and kiss me. |
| ANNA | You're not even going to lock (the door?) Right, it (doesn't lock) D'you need to pretend I'm an organist? |
| WESLEY | No. |
| ANNA | But I should keep the gown on, right? |

| | |
|---|---|
| WESLEY | No. |
| ANNA | I could take it off and put it on a few times — and you could call it foreplay. |

[WESLEY *pulls* ANNA *to him and they begin kissing passionately. Eventually, however, she pushes him away.*]

Hey. Hey.

[ANNA *is sitting up.*]

| | |
|---|---|
| | Dang. |
| WESLEY | What! |
| ANNA | I can't do it. Damn. Damn. I just can't. I can't put your career in jeopardy. |
| WESLEY | That's okay (don't worry) |
| ANNA | No, this is too important to you |
| WESLEY | No one (will know) |
| ANNA | We'll know. |

[ANNA *is getting off* WESLEY.]

On Friday I was all set to do it on my desk but just two days later, on a Sunday afternoon, with all the odds favouring orgasm — I can't. I could have if you hadn't got all serious on me but there's too much at stake here, sorry.

[WESLEY *sits up. Pause.*]

| | |
|---|---|
| WESLEY | I think I can apologize now. |
| ANNA | It won't make a difference. I just can't do it here. |
| WESLEY | No — I mean, I just had one of those blinding flashes on the road to Damascus things. |

| | |
|---|---|
| ANNA | When. |
| WESLEY | When you were climbing off me. It was sort of like a petit mal ethics seizure. I understand. What was wrong. About Friday. You were right. |

[ANNA *kisses* WESLEY. *She is interrupted by:*]

| | |
|---|---|
| JASON | *(Outside door.)* Hello? |
| ANNA | Who's that? |
| JASON | *(Knocking.)* Hello? |
| ANNA | It's Jason! |
| WESLEY | *(Calling.)* Just a minute. |
| ANNA | Get rid of him! |
| WESLEY | *(Calling.)* Go away! |
| JASON | What!? |
| WESLEY | Come back later! *(Points to the closet.)* In there! |
| JASON | I'd like to see you now. |
| WESLEY | Hold on. |

[JASON *enters.* ANNA *is in the closet.*]

| | |
|---|---|
| JASON | This won't take long. |
| WESLEY | Jason! |
| JASON | I guess you're surprised to see me. |
| WESLEY | A little. |
| JASON | I want to talk to you. |
| WESLEY | Here? |
| JASON | I didn't know where else to find you. |
| WESLEY | You want to talk right now? |
| JASON | Why not. |
| WESLEY | Wouldn't you rather make an appointment for tomorrow? |
| JASON | I'm flying to Toronto tonight so it (has to be) |

| | |
|---|---|
| WESLEY | But I just had a (service and I'm) |
| JASON | I know. It's Sunday. *(Beat.)* What were you doing just now? |
| WESLEY | Praying. |
| JASON | It sounded like you were talking to someone. |
| WESLEY | I was praying in tongues. |
| JASON | I don't know what that means. |
| WESLEY | I was channeling God, how's that. |
| JASON | No wonder you get along with Mom. She still sleeps under a pyramid. |
| WESLEY | I really don't like people barging in on me. |
| JASON | This won't take long. |
| WESLEY | How long is not long? |
| JASON | Three minutes. |
| WESLEY | Okay, you've got three minutes. Have a seat. Better yet, let's go down the street and have a coffee. |
| JASON | I don't want to interrupt your day any more than I have to. Sundays are your big day, right. |
| WESLEY | Yeah, there's the preaching thing and then the hospital-visiting thing and if I get it all done the treat myself to a movie thing. *(Suddenly the thought strikes him:)* Gosh — I'm sorry. You've come to me with something and I'm being flippant — is there something I can help you with, are you in (trouble or) |
| JASON | I wanted to apologize. |
| WESLEY | Yes, that's today's theme. |
| JASON | Huh? |
| WESLEY | Never mind. |
| JASON | I was rude to you on Friday. I thought about it all weekend. Well, some of the weekend. |
| WESLEY | That's right — you had a date. |
| JASON | Yeah. My first date with a lawyer. It gave me |

|          | insight into what it must've been like for the guys dating Mom. Lawyers are really neurotic. |
| WESLEY   | Your mother isn't the slightest bit neurotic! |
| JASON    | Excuse me? She's like the textbook for it. |
| WESLEY   | She's a very grounded person. |
| JASON    | You haven't seen her in ten years. |
| WESLEY   | What's your point. |

[JASON *pulls judgment out of his pocket.*]

| JASON  | This case she's ruling on. |
| WESLEY | Is that what I think it is? |
| JASON  | It's her final notes. |
| WESLEY | That's her — *(For* ANNA*'s benefit; outside the closet:)* Let the record show, Jason has just produced a bootleg copy of the Sophie Jamieson decision. |
| JASON  | Tomorrow she is going into court and she's going to grant an injunction forcing the government to give that woman heart surgery. |
| WESLEY | Really? |
| JASON  | Yes. |
| WESLEY | She's doing it. |
| JASON  | This is hardly a surprise to you. |
| WESLEY | Well I knew her leanings but she hadn't got the (case law) |
| JASON  | Two days ago she hadn't made up her mind. At least not like this. This is like an editorial for a — student newspaper, it's lefter than left; she's going to make a complete ass of herself. As well as an incorrect decision. Which is going to put a cloud over her career. Now — how could this happen? Two plus two — you just showed up. |
| WESLEY | Oh for God's sake — what do you take me |

|          |                                                                 |
|----------|-----------------------------------------------------------------|
|          | because I understood she was doing it for me, it was truly an immense sacrifice — |
| WESLEY   | She might have been doing it for herself. Oh, the egotism of youth. I've got a meeting in a few minutes. Get to your point. |
| JASON    | My point? I love her. A lot. I don't have any other family. I don't know if she told you, but Gran died just before Christmas — so it's just Mom and me. And I know it's "sexist" to be protective of her but I don't care. That's how I am with her. And she's good at some things, like the law, but when it comes to men, she's hopeless. You haven't seen the guys she's dated. |
| WESLEY   | There you go again! |
| JASON    | She doesn't know what slimebuckets men are. She's still in that hippie time warp, you know, when you guys all sat around playing recorders and bodypainting and doing macramé. |
| WESLEY   | We never did macramé! |
| JASON    | My dad did. When Mom met him he was teaching macramé at the Y. |

[WESLEY *shrugs*.]

|          |                                                                 |
|----------|-----------------------------------------------------------------|
|          | On a government grant! |
| WESLEY   | Jason, we did a whole lot of dumb things on grants in those days — macramé was the least of it. Do you really believe there are no decent men out there? |
| JASON    | If there are, she hasn't met them. |
| WESLEY   | Are you decent? |
| JASON    | Not always. |
| WESLEY   | Well, I'm pretty decent. |
| JASON    | Is that what they think at your old church? |

| | |
|---|---|
| WESLEY | *(Kicking closet door.)* How'd you know that? |
| JASON | Mom told me, yesterday. And by the way — nice eye. You get that from an organist's husband? |
| WESLEY | Your mother has a big mouth. |
| JASON | She also told me you came to her office pretending to be interested in her, but you were actually there to check out her take on the Jamieson case. |
| WESLEY | Anna and I have (resolved this) |
| JASON | You're no good for her! You weren't last time and you aren't now. When you took off last time |
| WESLEY | IT WAS TEN GODDAMN YEARS AGO GET A LIFE! |
| JASON | YOU GET A LIFE! AND STAY OUT OF HERS! |
| WESLEY | How long are you going to carry this (around with you) |
| JASON | When you took off that was the only time I ever saw her cry, ever. It was the only time I ever saw her actually fall apart, always she'd pretended to be this tough cookie, protecting me and Gran. And then you slide a note under the door, a shitty little note because you're too gutless to come around and talk to us — which would have been the "decent" thing to do. So there she is, completely unhinged and — do you know how scary that is? |
| WESLEY | It's ancient (history) |
| JASON | Yeah, it was ten years ago. I know: I'm an idiot, a sexist idiot to even think about it. I guess I'm an idiot to care enough about her to try and stop it happening again. I'd started calling you "Dad" you know. |
| WESLEY | You never did. (That's a lie) |

| | |
|---|---|
| JASON | Not to your face. I wasn't that brave. But at school. Stupid eh. I didn't realize yet that people came into your lives and then stuck a note under your door and that was it. Stay away from her. |
| WESLEY | If you're done, go. Get the hell out of here. |
| JASON | You're ordering me out. |
| WESLEY | Damn right I am. |
| JASON | This is a change. Usually you're the one who leaves. |
| WESLEY | Goodbye you little cretin. You're a disgrace. You know something? I'm glad I walked out on you ten years ago. If I'd had to spend time watching you grow up like — that — I think I might've murdered you sometime along the way! You're a disgrace! You're a disgrace to our education system, to our — community — you're a disgrace to your mother! |

[ANNA *bursts out of the closet.*]

| | |
|---|---|
| ANNA | No, he's not! |
| JASON | Where the hell did you come from! |
| ANNA | He's not a disgrace. |
| WESLEY | Oh yes (he is) |
| JASON | Mom! |
| ANNA | I'm proud of him. Really proud. |
| WESLEY | Of that! |
| JASON | MOM! |
| ANNA | Because he's worked hard (and) |
| WESLEY | He's a little Nazi. |
| ANNA | Don't you ever call him that! He's just young and really certain about things but he'll loosen up, you said that (yourself) |
| JASON | Don't patronize me! |
| WESLEY | I can't believe you're defending him! |

| | |
|---|---|
| ANNA | He's my son! |
| WESLEY | He's also an adult. *(To* JASON:*)* And your values suck. |
| ANNA | Leave him alone! |
| JASON | *(Pause.)* Do you want to tell me what the hell you're doing here? |
| ANNA | After you, my beloved son. |
| JASON | I asked you first. |
| ANNA | Youth before "flakes." |
| JASON | Where'd you come from? *(Looking.)* It's a closet! |
| ANNA | *(Looking too.)* Good Lord, you're right. |
| JASON | You were in there. |
| ANNA | Yes. |
| JASON | The whole time. |
| ANNA | Yes. |
| JASON | So — you guys playing hide and seek? |
| WESLEY | I realize this is not the most dignified situation. |
| JASON | Oh, don't let that stop you, Your Holiness. |
| WESLEY | Don't you get sarcastic with me! |
| ANNA | Jason, none of this is any of your business. I was conferring with Wesley and I wish I hadn't hidden when you came, because maybe then I wouldn't have overheard you saying all those stupid things. |
| WESLEY | See, you're not proud of him! |
| ANNA | I'm proud he's got opinions. Now stay out of this! *(To* JASON.*)* To deal with the minor points: I've gone out with many decent men in my time. And as far as dating slimebuckets, yes, I've done that too, but you don't need to spread that around. Nor do I like you coming to my friend's office and telling him I'm neurotic. *(Beat.)* Am I? |
| JASON | Well yes (you are) |
| ANNA | THAT WAS A JOKE DAMMIT!! I'm not |

neurotic, I'm too paranoid to be neurotic!

WESLEY    You're not paranoid!

ANNA    That was another joke!

WESLEY    I knew that. *(To* JASON*:)* She's completely grounded.

ANNA    I thought I told you to stay out of this.

WESLEY    It's my office!

ANNA    Well you shut the hell up or I'll do your other eye.

WESLEY    Okay okay I'll leave.

ANNA    STAY — it's your office!

JASON    You gave him that black eye!?

ANNA    Yes.

JASON    *(Lunging at* WESLEY*:)* What the hell were you doing to her!

ANNA    *(Getting in between them.)* JASON! GROW UP!

JASON    What did he do to you?!

WESLEY    I wasn't doing anything to her. And if you lay one hand on me I'll haul you both up on assault.

[JASON *and* ANNA *stand together; united. It almost looks as if they'll both deck* WESLEY. *Pause.*]

JASON    Mom.

ANNA    What.

JASON    Do you want to explain why you're wearing his gown?

ANNA    *(Beat.)* No.

JASON    Are you going to tell me why you were hiding in his closet?

ANNA    *(Pause.)* No.

JASON    *(Points to panties on floor.)* Are those yours?

ANNA    Of course not, don't be ridiculous. Those are some woman's panties. They could be

|          | anybody's. You know his reputation. He's a slut! |
|----------|---|
| WESLEY   | *(Pokes at them with his foot.)* They're way too small to be your mother's. With her hips?! |
| ANNA     | All right, they're mine! |
| JASON    | It's kind of hard to take either of you seriously when I come in here and you're in there and that's lying there and you're wearing that and he's covering up and |
| WESLEY   | It wasn't like you think. |
| ANNA     | It was exactly like you think. But what you don't know is that I was using the promise of sexual intercourse to make a legitimate point with him about the independence of the judiciary. |

[*They all stop and think about this.*]

|          |   |
|----------|---|
| WESLEY   | You were? |
| ANNA     | Shut up. |
| WESLEY   | Wait: are you telling me that all along you were planning to get me up on that desk? |
| ANNA     | DO YOU MIND!? |
| WESLEY   | YES!! |
| ANNA     | At the time of my mounting the desk I had no ulterior motives. |
| WESLEY   | Well that's good because (I don't like being used) |
| JASON    | WHAT DO YOU SEE IN HIM! |
| ANNA     | Don't yell at me. |
| WESLEY   | You want to know what she (sees in me) |
| ANNA     | SHUT UP! |
| WESLEY   | Okay, that does it. Either I get to talk — or I leave. |
| ANNA     | You have to stay. You're getting buzzed. |

[JASON *registers "buzzed."*]

Jason: I'm a grown woman. I can see whoever I want,  whenever I want.

JASON         So you're "seeing" him now.

WESLEY        (We are?)

ANNA          We were about to see. What we could see. Or maybe we were going to see a bit now and see a whole lot later, and maybe not actually here but yes, there was a good chance something very magical was going to happen today between two people for whom there has been precious little magic.

JASON         He's just using you.

ANNA          You want to know something? I want to be used. I would love to be used. I haven't been used in so goddamn long I wouldn't know the difference between a naked man and a lumpy shag rug with mildew.

[*Everyone pauses to visualize that.*]

Anyway, even if he is using me for sex — isn't that exactly what you told me men do?

JASON         It isn't just sex he wants. He's making you change your decision.

ANNA          I haven't changed a thing. I know where he stands, he knows where I stand. *(Snatches judgment back.)* Restricting access to medical care is illegal.

WESLEY        (Immoral.)

ANNA          Illegal, end of argument.

JASON         Even if it preserves the health care system itself.

ANNA          The minute you lop someone out of it, there is no "system."

JASON         *(One more time, as if to morons:)* If we want

|           | basic medical care for everyone then we've got to restrict specialized care to some. It's really not a difficult concept. |
| ANNA      | But why is it so difficult for you to grasp that if it's possible to save a life — we must. Because the law requires us to treat everyone equally and that (includes the elderly) |
| WESLEY    | Or because applying "cost-benefit analysis" to human lives is defeatist and selfish — and immoral. |
| ANNA      | *(To* WESLEY.*)* Shut up. *(To* JASON.*)* Where are you going? |
| JASON     | *(Leaving.)* Forget it. |
| ANNA      | Don't just walk out! |
| JASON     | You guys don't get it. |
| WESLEY    | *(Disgusted.)* We "don't get it." |
| JASON     | I'm selfish. I'm immoral. Gee, I wish I could've been in your generation. You're such saints, and we're all scuzzbags. So here you guys are: a judge who hides in closets and you, a Man of God who bedhops and gets buzzed. |

[WESLEY *and* ANNA *look perplexed, then laugh.*]

What's so funny.

[WESLEY *and* ANNA *continue laughing, and speak over each other.*]

| WESLEY | You were thinking |
| ANNA   | He's not getting "buzzed" as buzzed — drunk |
| WESLEY | It's buzzed as in called to a meeting |
| ANNA   | His hiring committee |
| WESLEY | They're meeting in the park |

| | |
|---|---|
| ANNA | To approve him |
| WESLEY | Hopefully approve me and then they'll come back here |
| ANNA | And (buzz him.) |
| WESLEY | Buzz me. |
| JASON | May I continue? Do you want to giggle some more. |
| ANNA | Sorry. |
| JASON | *(Resuming.)* You always lectured me on being an adult … |

[JASON *pauses; waiting for* ANNA *and* WESLEY *to stop laughing.*]

You said being an adult meant making difficult choices and gradually I've come to see that, yes, it's true, if it's easy it's likely wrong — or maybe right for some but wrong for others. But the minute you have to face a reality that is inconvenient or hurtful or actually involves making a hard choice — you run and hide behind whatever "principles" or "ideals" you've managed to trump up to suit the situation. So hey — let's bankrupt ourselves with a million heart operations because God knows we're too gutless to consider the alternative. And then — just when you're cornered — just when someone is forcing you to actually consider the fact that we can't give children proper school lunches because the Sophie Jamiesons of the world won't sell her house to pay for her new arteries — well, somehow, through some miracle of middle-aged logic, it's me who's greedy, me who's selfish, me who can't face reality.

| | |
|---|---|
| WESLEY | So all the cutbacks we've endured over the past decade aren't enough. |
| JASON | No! |
| ANNA | Or the fact we've licked the deficit? |
| JASON | We haven't touched the debt! Nor for that matter have we dealt with your indexed pension! |
| WESLEY | Nor are we properly taxing the corporations! |
| JASON | And how much tax does this place pay? Aw Jesus, what's the use. *(To* ANNA.*)* I wish you'd stop sometime and really take a look at me, really look, and while you're doing that, try thinking about what the world looks like through my eyes. All my life I've wished for that, that you'd stop for one minute and entertain the idea that the road you're travelling might have parallel lines, or ones going this way or that way and maybe they're okay, too, and maybe the girls I date aren't all sluts — or fakers — and maybe the job I landed after working so goddamn hard isn't just an excuse for lame jokes. Maybe I'm SCARED about the job. Maybe I'm SCARED SHITLESS I'm going to screw up. Maybe I'd like some support from you Mom NOT MONEY, SUPPORT and I'm sorry it's a bank BUT IT'S A BANK! *(Holds his hands out one above the other, indicating they've been on separate planes.)* We've spent our whole lives going like this. We've never connected unless I made the effort. God Mom, didn't you ever notice it was Gran I told everything to? |
| ANNA | Of course I noticed. |
| JASON | Well she's dead now, Mom. And I don't have anyone who listens. |

go and at least talk to him, okay?

[ANNA *is hesitating.*]

|        |   |
|--------|---|
| | Please. Just go. |
| ANNA | Okay. Okay. I don't know what I'm going to say but — *(Going to the door.)* Wait. *(Stops; returns; goes to purse.)* |
| WESLEY | What're you doing? Go! |

[ANNA *has fished the judgment out of her purse.*]

| | |
|--------|---|
| ANNA | Here. You may as well read it — everyone else has. |

[ANNA *hurries out. WESLEY slumps back on his desk. He tidies it a bit. He puts ANNA's clothing in a pile. Then he picks up the judgment and sits down to read it.*]

| | |
|--------|---|
| WESLEY | "The Premier is a (fascist asshole)" |

[WESLEY *bursts into laughter; he reads on. ANNA bursts back in.*]

| | |
|--------|---|
| | Why're you back! |
| ANNA | Why'd you send me out in this!? |
| WESLEY | Where's Jason? |
| ANNA | LOOK WHAT I'M WEARING! |
| WESLEY | You look fine to me — where is he? |
| ANNA | No listen listen, Wes, you don't understand. I got outside and there was a group of people sitting in the park across the road. How many are there on your probation committee? |
| WESLEY | Four. |

| | |
|---|---|
| ANNA | How many of them are really fat? |
| WESLEY | Four. |
| ANNA | How many have grey hair? |
| WESLEY | Four. So it was them. *(Not worried.)* They saw you run out of the church with robes on. Were they even awake? |
| ANNA | Oh they were awake and when I tell you what happened next you won't be smiling. |
| WESLEY | Why. |
| ANNA | There was a breeze. |
| WESLEY | Oh. |
| ANNA | It was the Devil. He was blowing some hot air down the street and it got under these nice, light, airy robes of yours and — |
| WESLEY | Ahh. |
| ANNA | Yeah. I'm standing there across from your probation officers and well that breeze went *(Indicates up.)* |
| WESLEY | How far up? |
| ANNA | Over my face up. |

[WESLEY *begins to laugh.*]

| | |
|---|---|
| | How can you laugh! |
| WESLEY | *(Picking up the panties.)* I'm enjoying the image. |

[WESLEY *is laughing, but* ANNA *is not. She starts getting dressed under the gown.*]

| | |
|---|---|
| WESLEY | I'm sorry, it's just (funny) |
| ANNA | They hold your future in their hands |
| WESLEY | Maybe they didn't see. |
| ANNA | They must've. |
| WESLEY | There's still no connection to me. *(Sees* ANNA *is not sharing in the laughter.)* What. |
| ANNA | There's something else. |

WESLEY       What.
ANNA         Jason was with them.
WESLEY       Oh.
ANNA         Yeah.
WESLEY       Oh.
ANNA         I'm sorry. I'm truly, truly sorry.

[WESLEY *shrugs.*]

How can you be so calm!
WESLEY       There's nothing much I can do, is there.
             I've had three wonderful months here. I've
             come to love these people. I think they
             respect me. If they change their minds
             because of something Jason is telling them,
             well, then I guess I'm better off leaving.
             *(Holds up judgment.)* And I'll have this to
             cheer me. This is very brave, Anna. I don't
             know about the first line, though.
ANNA         That's just my motivation.
WESLEY       When do you deliver it?
ANNA         Ten, tomorrow.
WESLEY       I'll be there. I'll be there with Sophie's
             daughter. Hell, I'll bring the whole
             congregation — unless I've been banished.
             You're going to get your first standing
             ovation. Thank you. Thank you, Anna. But
             now you've got to go. You've still got to
             make it up with him.
ANNA         I know. I'll just get dressed.

[*There's a buzz.* WESLEY *and* ANNA *look
at the intercom. There's another buzz.*]
WESLEY       That's them. (Goes to intercom.) Hello?
             Hello!

[*There's static.*]

| | |
|---|---|
| WESLEY | Right, it never works. Okay. Okay. It's showtime. |
| ANNA | I'm so sorry about Jason. |
| WESLEY | It's okay. |
| ANNA | I could come and explain (to them) |
| WESLEY | No. It's okay. *(Goes to door.)* Do you pray? |
| ANNA | No but I have crystals. Come back here a sec. Let me fix your collar. |

[WESLEY *returns.* ANNA *fixes his tie and then kisses him.*]

| | |
|---|---|
| ANNA | Good luck. |

[WESLEY *turns and leaves.* ANNA *starts to finish dressing. She tries to lock the door; realizes she can't. She looks around and goes into the closet to finish. After a second,* WESLEY *bursts back in — perhaps for another kiss or perhaps to chuck it all and not face the Hiring Committee. He sees that* ANNA *has gone, so he leaves again.* ANNA *comes out of the closet just as* JASON *walks in. He is holding some flowers.*]

| | |
|---|---|
| JASON | I stole them. |
| ANNA | Not from the church. |
| JASON | From the park. Where's Wesley? *(Indicates closet.)* |
| ANNA | No, he's upstairs with his Hiring Committee. We have to talk. Everything you said was right, I mean about me not listening. We should talk (about that) oh God Jason how could you! How could you go over there and talk to them! His career is hanging in the balance, you (have no right) |
| JASON | Mom Mom (Mom calm down) |

| | |
|---|---|
| ANNA | I don't care (if you hate him) |
| JASON | What were you just saying about listening to me? |
| ANNA | I was (saying that) |
| JASON | Well start listening! |
| ANNA | Yeah (but Jason) |
| JASON | Right now. Okay? When I left here, I ran out and I was cutting across the park and I saw them sitting there and I remembered who they were. So I was going to go and talk to them, I was going to say something about Wesley. I was. And I would've been justified. But well, they'd seen me come out of the church and they saw I was upset and they smiled at me, kind of like Gran. I mean, they all looked like Gran. Even the man looked like Gran. They asked if I'd been getting counselling from Wesley. And then before I could answer, well, they started telling me how much they, how much they love him. You should've heard them. They said it's the first time they felt someone really cared about them. Apparently he's a pathetic preacher, he makes them all fall asleep. He's so bad they had to move the coffee hour to before the service! But they said that until Wesley came they felt abandoned — being old — and I remembered that that was what Gran said, she used to say that she felt completely alone. |
| ANNA | She said that? |
| JASON | Yeah. |
| ANNA | She told you that. |

[JASON *nods*.]

She never said that to me.

| | |
|---|---|
| JASON | And then you came running out. And then your robes blew up. Mom: there's some things a son should never see. |
| ANNA | Or Hiring Committees. Oh, I must've blown it for him. |
| JASON | No — no — we got lucky. They never saw! The women were all sitting facing away from the church. |
| ANNA | But the old guy? |
| JASON | He turned to me and asked me if I'd seen anything unusual just then. And I said, "No sir." Like I'm going to say: "Yeah, pal, we just got flashed by my Mother." And he said it was too bad I hadn't seen what he had — because he'd just seen absolute proof there's a God. So I think Wesley's okay, I mean, I know he is. *(Pause.)* But I'm still not saying he's right for you. |
| ANNA | Fine. |
| JASON | And I'm not apologizing for anything I believe. |
| ANNA | Neither am I. |
| JASON | Okay. |
| ANNA | Fine. |
| JASON | Fine. I stand by everything I said. |
| ANNA | Me too. I stand by the judgment I'm giving tomorrow. |
| JASON | Sure. Even though it's wrong. |
| ANNA | *(Rolling her eyes.)* Even though it's wrong. |
| JASON | Fine. And I am proud of you. |
| ANNA | Ditto. |
| JASON | So we're being sappy, right? |
| ANNA | Yeah. |
| JASON | Good. Hold the mood. |
| ANNA | You want to do lunch? |
| JASON | Just us? |
| ANNA | Just us. |

JASON          You're on.

               [ANNA *takes the flowers. She turns, as if to leave, and then turns back and puts the flowers on* WESLEY*'s desk.* JASON *rolls his eyes. And then* ANNA *takes* JASON*'s hand and they leave. Black.*]

               **The End.**

Printed in the USA
CPSIA information can be obtained
at www.ICGtesting.com
JSHW012056140824
68134JS00035B/3478